Stay with it, SNOOPY

Selected cartoons from

SUMMERS WALK, WINTERS FLY

Vol. 3

by CHARLES M. SCHULZ

FAWCETT CREST • NEW YORK

STAY WITH IT, SNOOPY

This book prepared especially for Fawcett Crest Books, a unit of CBS Publications, the Consumer Publishing Division of CBS Inc. comprises a portion of SUMMERS FLY, WINTERS WALK and is reprinted by arrangement with Holt, Rinehart and Winston, Inc.

Contents of Book: PEANUTS® comic strips by Charles M. Schulz
Copyright © 1976, 1977 by United Feature Syndicate, Inc.

ISBN: 0-449-24310-9

Printed in the United States of America

First Fawcett Crest Printing: July 1980

10   9   8   7   6   5   4   3   2   1

Stay with it, SNOOPY

WELL, I FAILED AGAIN!

I THOUGHT I COULD EARN SOME MONEY FOR CHRISTMAS BY RAKING LEAVES, BUT NO ONE WOULD HIRE ME...

I GUESS THAT MEANS I CAN'T BUY ANY CHRISTMAS PRESENTS THIS YEAR...

IF YOU SOLD THE RAKE, YOU COULD AT LEAST BUY ME SOMETHING!

Napoleon was ready to leave for Moscow.

He kissed his wife, and whispered farewell.

As he rode off to battle, she shouted, "Don't get blown apart, Bonapart!"

WELL, SHE MIGHT HAVE SAID IT!

Mr. Claus
℅ North Pole

Dear Joe,

JOE?

HE HATES TO BE CALLED "SANTA"!

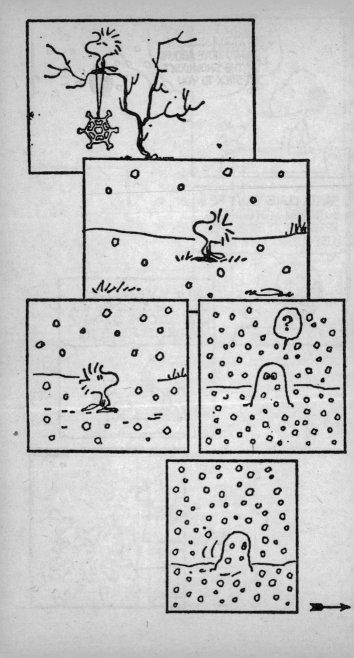

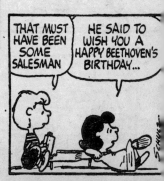

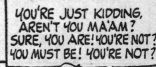

I'D LIKE TO READ THIS BOOK, MARCIE, BUT I'M KIND OF AFRAID

I HAD A GRANDFATHER WHO DIDN'T THINK MUCH OF READING...

HE ALWAYS SAID THAT IF YOU READ TOO MANY BOOKS, YOUR HEAD WOULD FALL OFF...

YOU START THE FIRST CHAPTER, SIR, AND I'LL HOLD ONTO YOUR HEAD!

SCHULZ

THE INTENTION, OF COURSE, IS TO CONTRAST A PLACE OF HUMAN LODGING WITH A PLACE FOR FEEDING ANIMALS

"PEACE AMONG MEN WITH WHOM HE IS PLEASED" IS AN INTERESTING TRANSLATION.. IT INDICATES THAT DIVINE PEACE IS NOT DEPENDENT ON HUMAN ATTITUDES...

THE NAME "BETHLEHEM" IS INTERESTING, TOO... IT MEANS "HOUSE OF BREAD.." I THINK THINGS LIKE THIS ARE FASCINATING...WHAT DO YOU THINK?

I THINK IF I DON'T GET EVERYTHING I WANT FOR CHRISTMAS THIS YEAR, I'M GONNA GROSS OUT!

SCHULZ

ALL RIGHT, MARCIE...WHAT BOOK SHOULD I READ?

HOW ABOUT ONE BY KATHERINE ANNE PORTER, OR JOYCE CAROL OATES OR PAMELA HANSFORD JOHNSON?

FORGET IT MARCIE... ALL THOSE AUTHORS HAVE THREE NAMES...

BY THE TIME I FINISHED READING THE AUTHOR'S NAME, I'D BE TOO TIRED TO READ THE BOOK!

YOU'RE REALLY WEIRD, SIR!

YOU MAY CHOOSE, IF YOU SO WISH, TO THROW THAT SNOWBALL AT ME...

YOU ALSO MAY CHOOSE, IF YOU SO WISH, NOT TO THROW THAT SNOWBALL AT ME...

OW, IF YOU CHOOSE TO RROW THAT SNOWBALL T ME, I WILL POUND YOU RIGHT INTO THE GROUND!

IF YOU CHOOSE NOT TO THROW THAT SNOWBALL AT ME, YOUR HEAD WILL BE SPARED

LIFE IS FULL OF CHOICES, BUT YOU NEVER GET ANY!

SCHULZ

THERE'S NOTHING WRONG WITH READING CEREAL BOXES...

SOME OF THE BEST STORIES I'VE EVER READ WERE ON CEREAL BOXES...AND YOU DON'T HAVE TO TURN ANY PAGES!

I PREDICT THAT SOME DAY A CEREAL BOX WILL WIN THE PULITZER PRIZE!

SEE, MARCIE? I DID IT!

YOU'RE WEIRD, SIR...

BE CAREFUL, LINUS...YOU'RE GOING TO FALL!

I DON'T THINK I CAN GET DOWN...IT'S TOO SLIPPERY...

'M LEAVING ON THE SCHOOL 'US, LINUS, BUT DON'T WORRY! 'LL SEND A HELICOPTER 'OR YOU! BE BRAVE, MY SWEET BABBOO!

HELICOPTER?

"SWEET BABBOO"?

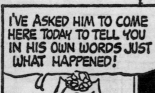

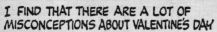

IF YOU PUT YOUR SUPPER DISH TO YOUR EAR, YOU CAN HEAR THE SOUNDS OF A RESTAURANT...

I CAN EVEN HEAR A WAITER TALKING...

"I'M SORRY SIR... WE DON'T ACCEPT CREDIT CARDS!"

WOODSTOCK AND HIS FRIEND ARE TALKING ABOUT ME...

I KNOW JUST WHAT THEY'RE SAYING...

THEY FORGET THAT I CAN READ BEAKS!

PEANUTS

YOU'RE A PAL, SNOOPY!
(selected cartoons from
You Need Help Charlie Brown, Vol. 2)   23775-3 $1.2:

PLAY BALL, SNOOPY
(selected cartoons from
Win a Few, Lose a Few, Charlie Brown, Vol. 1)
                                                 23222-0 $1.2

YOU'VE GOT TO BE KIDDING, SNOOPY!
(selected cartoons from
Speak Softly and Carry a Beagle, Vol. 1)   23453-3 $1.2:

HERE'S TO YOU, CHARLIE BROWN
(selected cartoons from
You Can't Win, Charlie Brown, Vol. 2) •   23708-7 $1.2:

HEY, PEANUTS!
(selected cartoons from
More Peanuts, Vol. II)   24013-4 $1.2.

                                                          800